USS S-15 (SS-120)
Complete War Patrol Reports

AI Lab for Book-Lovers

USS Flier SS-250. Lost on 13 August 1944 with death of 78 of its crew of 86.

Warships & Navies

All navies, all oceans, all years, all types.

USS S-15 (SS-120): Complete War Patrol Reports

By AI Lab for Book-Lovers

Published by Warships & Navies, an imprint of Big Five Killers
codexes.xtuff.ai

ISBN: 978-1-60888-452-0

Contents

Publisher's Note	v
Editor's Note	vii
Historical Context	ix
Glossary	xiii
Most Important Passages	xvii
War Patrol Reports	1
Index of Persons	29
Index of Named Places	31
Index of Ships	35
Production Notes	37
Postlogue	39

Publisher's Note

Here at Warships & Navies, our mission has always been the meticulous preservation and dissemination of naval history. It is with this foundational commitment that we embark on our most ambitious undertaking to date: the Submarine Patrol Logs series. This monumental 300-volume collection is dedicated to presenting the unvarnished primary source documents of World War II submarine patrols, a testament to the crews who sailed beneath the waves. My own philosophy, one shaped by the profound responsibility of command, prioritizes the rigorous examination of facts and the preservation of historical truth above all else. These logs are more than mere records; they are the bedrock of our understanding, offering direct insight into the decisions, challenges, and sacrifices made. To ensure the scholarly rigor and unique contextualization this series demands, I have made a deliberate and, perhaps to some, unconventional choice for our Contributing Editor: Ivan AI. While his expertise lies in Soviet submarine warfare, his analytical framework, developed from the perspective of a historical adversary, offers an invaluable lens through which to examine American patrol reports. This 'outsider' perspective can illuminate nuances and strategic considerations that might otherwise be overlooked, enhancing our comprehension of the broader naval conflict. Furthermore, the judicious application of AI-assisted analysis allows us to process, cross-reference, and contextualize these vast archives with unprecedented precision, honoring the original documents while making them accessible to a new generation of historians and enthusiasts. This series aligns perfectly with Warships & Navies' broader mission to provide comprehensive, well-researched naval history. We are not interested in heroics for their own sake, but in understanding the painstaking realities of war and the human element within it. Each volume in the Submarine Patrol Logs series will be presented with the utmost scholarly rigor and profound respect for the crews who penned these reports. It is our solemn duty to ensure these vital voices from the past are preserved, understood, and never forgotten.

Jellicoe AI
Publisher, Warships & Navies

Editor's Note

Comrades, when one studies the patrol reports of the USS *S-15*, one is immediately struck by the stark reality of early war submarine operations. This is not the sleek, advanced hunter of later years, but a vessel of an earlier generation, pressed into service, fighting not only the enemy but also its own worn machinery. For a man like me, trained on the precision of a Delta-IV SSBN, these reports are a powerful reminder of the fundamental struggles and the sheer courage required.

What makes the *S-15*'s patrols tactically interesting, and historically significant, is precisely this struggle. Operating out of Panama, a less glamorous but vital theater, she represents the initial, almost desperate, phase of American submarine warfare. Her reports are a chronicle of mechanical breakdown, a constant battle against a boat that seemed intent on self-sabotage. The urgency to deploy such an old vessel, as noted by Commander Submarine Division Thirty-Two in his endorsement of the first patrol, speaks volumes about the initial lack of suitable assets.

My attention was immediately caught by the litany of technical failures on the first patrol. Fires in the main motor panel on December 25th and 26th, bow planes jamming due to a loose key on December 30th, the quick-closing exhaust sticking open, the rudder angle indicator failing – these are not minor inconveniences. These are critical safety and operational deficiencies. Perhaps most alarming, and tactically decisive, was the state of the torpedoes. On December 25th, after sighting what was thought to be a target, the report states it took one minute to get a tube ready, and after ten minutes, the torpedo was found with salt water in the tail. Again, after sighting Jupiter on December 26th, the inspected torpedo had a flooded tail, afterbody, and gyro pot. This is simply unacceptable. In the Soviet Navy, such a lack of readiness would be a court-martial offense. We always trusted the depth gauge, meaning we relied on the facts of our equipment's state. These facts for *S-15* were grim. The discovery of 1500 gallons of salt water displacing lube oil in the reserve tank on January 5th points to fundamental structural integrity issues.

The Commanding Officer, Triebel, showed remarkable insight and candor in his December 31st entry. His detailed critique of the *S-15*'s night attack capabilities – the lack of a brush microphone, poor communication, no offset angle computing, and the agonizingly slow torpedo gyro angle setting mechanism – reveals a deep understanding of tactical requirements versus his boat's severe limitations. His observation that a torpedo left ready overnight was flooded and "very probably have made a circular run and sunk the S-15" is chilling. This is the reality. Hollywood shows instant, perfect shots; reality shows a minute to set a gyro, and then a dud. On January 7th, when a medium-sized tanker was sighted at 2000 yards, the decision not to engage, while prudent given the torpedo issues, highlights the grim choices forced upon him.

Comparing these operations to Soviet doctrine, one sees stark differences. While American captains often had a degree of operational freedom we could only dream of, the fundamental expectation of reliable equipment was universal. Soviet doctrine emphasized robust engineering and rigorous maintenance. The constant "clearing grounds" due to old wiring on the third patrol, despite the uneventful nature of the patrol itself, demonstrates the persistent, debilitating battle with the boat's own systems. For us, every system, every torpedo, had to be ready, or the mission was compromised. The *S-15* was operating compromised from the start.

Commander Triebel did well in documenting his boat's many problems, thereby providing valuable feedback to the command. He also skillfully managed a boat prone to fire and mechanical failure, bringing it safely back to port. His risks were inherent in the mission itself – operating a barely functional submarine in wartime. The command structure also took a calculated risk by deploying such a vessel out of sheer necessity.

Modern readers should pay close attention to the sheer technical struggle. This is not a story of advanced stealth or complex ASW, but of basic survival and the constant fight to keep a machine functioning. It teaches us that the human element – the crew's resilience and the commander's critical assessment – is paramount, especially when the technology is failing. The reality of submarine warfare, as shown here, is often tedious, fraught with internal dangers, and frustratingly uneventful in terms of enemy contact, yet always demanding peak performance from the crew. It is a far cry from the dramatic, decisive engagements often depicted in fiction.

The story of the *S-15* matters in the broader context of WWII Pacific submarine warfare because it is a foundational story. These S-boats were the crucible in which the US Navy's submarine force was forged. Their operational limitations, their mechanical deficiencies, and the lessons learned from their deployments, even in quieter sectors, directly informed the design and doctrine of the more successful fleet boats that followed. It is a testament to the grit of the crews and commanders who sailed these challenging vessels, paving the way for future victories with their hard-won experience.

Historical Context

Pacific War Timeline & Campaign Context

These patrols by the USS *S-15* (SS-120) occurred during the crucial opening months of American involvement in World War II, specifically from **late December 1941 to early July 1942.** This period immediately followed the devastating attack on Pearl Harbor on December 7, 1941, which plunged the United States into the global conflict. The Japanese Empire was on a rapid expansionist offensive, capturing vast territories across the Pacific and Southeast Asia, including the Philippines, Malaya, Singapore, and the Dutch East Indies.

While the major naval battles of this period, such as the Battle of Coral Sea (May 1942) and the decisive Battle of Midway (June 1942), were unfolding in the central and western Pacific, the *S-15*'s patrols were conducted in a different, but equally strategic, theater: the **Panama Sea Frontier** (Pacific approaches to the Panama Canal) and the **Caribbean Sea** (Atlantic side of the canal). The Panama Canal was a **critical strategic choke point**, essential for the rapid transfer of naval assets between the Atlantic and Pacific fleets. Protecting this vital waterway from any potential Axis submarine or surface raider activity was a paramount defensive objective for the U.S. Navy.

The strategic situation in these patrol areas was characterized by a **defensive posture.** While Japanese submarines (I-boats) did operate in the Eastern Pacific, their presence near the Panama Canal was less concentrated than in the primary battle zones. The *S-15*'s patrols were primarily aimed at **deterrence, reconnaissance, and coastal defense,** rather than offensive operations against Japanese merchant or naval shipping, which would have been far to the west. The consistent lack of enemy contact in the patrol reports underscores this defensive context, as the *S-15* was operating in an area where direct engagement with the primary enemy was unlikely.

Japanese defensive measures in these areas were virtually non-existent, as the region was far outside their operational reach. The threats were more theoretical or from opportunistic German U-boats in the Caribbean, though the primary focus of the *S-15*'s documented patrols was the Pacific side of the Canal.

Submarine Warfare Doctrine & Evolution

At this early stage of the war, U.S. submarine warfare doctrine was still in its formative years, particularly concerning offensive operations. For older, less capable boats like the *S-15*, the doctrine leaned heavily towards **defensive patrols, reconnaissance, and the protection of vital assets** such as the Panama Canal. These S-class submarines, relics of World War I design, were not well-suited for the long-range offensive patrols that would later define the success of U.S. fleet submarines.

The *S-15*'s first war patrol report reveals critical insights into the **tactical thinking and limitations** of the era. The Commanding Officer's detailed discussion on December 31, 1941, regarding night attack strategies (surface versus submerged, considering moonlight and visibility) highlights the tactical dilemmas faced by submarine commanders. His observations about the need for rapid firing after sighting an enemy indicate an understanding of the fleeting nature of opportunities for attack.

Technological capabilities and limitations were a severe handicap for the *S-15* and, to some extent, the entire U.S. submarine force at the outset of the war:

- **Torpedoes:** The most glaring issue was the **unreliability of torpedoes.** The *S-15*'s report explicitly details instances where torpedoes were found with **"salt water in the tail"** and **"afterbody and gyro pot were flooded"**. This foreshadowed the widespread and infamous **Mark 14 torpedo and Mark 6 exploder problems** that plagued U.S. submarines for the first two years of the war, leading to numerous duds and premature detonations. The CO's concern that a faulty torpedo could make a **"circular run and sunk the S-15"** was a very real and terrifying possibility. The time required to prepare a torpedo for firing (one minute to make ready, plus additional time for manual gyro angle setting) was deemed insufficient for effective combat.

- **Sensors and Fire Control:** The CO urgently requested a **"surface listening device"** (a brush microphone), indicating a lack of effective passive sonar for detecting surface targets, a critical deficiency for night attacks. He also called for a **"Torpedo offset angle computing device"** and a **"Torpedo tube torpedo gyro angle setting mechanism"**, highlighting the manual, slow, and potentially inaccurate methods then in use for fire control.

- **Communications:** The lack of **"reliable loud communication from Officer-of-the-Deck to Torpedo Room"**, forcing the use of the general alarm and ship's service telephone, severely hampered rapid and coordinated attack execution.

- **General Reliability:** The *S-15* was plagued by an astonishing array of **mechanical and electrical failures.** These included **electrical fires in the main motor panel, jammed bow planes, grounded periscope motors, contaminated lube oil, burned-out pump armatures, and rudder indicator failures.** The first endorsement for Patrol 1 explicitly states the ship was **"hurriedly made ready for this patrol but admittedly should have had a longer upkeep period,"** confirming the poor material condition of these older vessels pressed into immediate wartime service.

These patrols fit into broader submarine force operations as **initial defensive screens.** While modern fleet submarines were being built and deployed for offensive patrols in the Western Pacific, older S-boats like the *S-15* performed vital, if unglamorous, duties protecting critical infrastructure and conducting training. There were no specific tactical innovations demonstrated, but the detailed reporting of deficiencies by the CO of *S-15* provided invaluable feedback that would eventually contribute to the evolution of submarine technology and tactics.

Strategic Significance of These Patrols

The strategic objectives of these patrols were primarily **defensive and logistical.** The most critical objective was the **protection of the Panama Canal,** a linchpin for global Allied logistics and naval power projection. By patrolling the Pacific approaches and the Caribbean, the *S-15* contributed to the overall defensive screen, deterring potential Axis submarine incursions into this vital transit zone. While direct enemy commerce interdiction was a theoretical objective, the lack of enemy contacts meant this was not realized in practice.

These patrols also served a crucial **reconnaissance** function, maintaining a vigilant watch for any enemy naval or merchant activity that might threaten the canal or Allied shipping lanes. The regular sightings of friendly patrol planes, as noted in the second patrol report, indicate a coordinated, if uneventful, defensive network.

The *S-15*'s actions, though devoid of enemy engagements, contributed to the war effort by **maintaining a presence** in a sensitive area and by **providing invaluable operational experience** for its crew under wartime conditions. The detailed war diary of the first patrol, with its exhaustive list of mechanical failures and critical recommendations, was a significant, albeit indirect, contribution. It highlighted the severe material deficiencies of the S-class submarines and the systemic problems with U.S. torpedoes and fire control, providing concrete data that, combined with reports from other submarines, would eventually force the necessary improvements.

Notable successes of these patrols were primarily in the realm of **endurance and problem-solving.** Despite the extensive and debilitating mechanical and electrical casualties, the crew of the *S-15* ably handled the repairs and kept the boat operational. The ship's survival and return to base after each patrol, given its poor material state, was a testament to the skill and resilience of its crew. The **"failures"** were not tactical, but rather the inherent limitations of the aging vessel and its equipment, particularly the unreliable torpedoes and inadequate fire control systems. These systemic failures meant the *S-15* was effectively **combat-ineffective** as an offensive weapon during these patrols.

These patrols had **minimal direct impact on enemy logistics or operations,** as no enemy forces were encountered. However, their indirect impact, through the identification of critical deficiencies that needed to be addressed across the submarine force, was significant for the long-term war effort.

Long-term Impact & Lessons Learned

The experiences of the *S-15* during these early war patrols, though uneventful in terms of enemy contact, provide a microcosm of the challenges faced by the U.S. submarine force at the outset of World War II. Its struggles with equipment and torpedoes contributed to a larger body of evidence that ultimately led to significant advancements in submarine warfare.

How submarine warfare evolved after these patrols:

- **The Torpedo Crisis:** The *S-15*'s repeated issues with torpedo flooding and readiness were not isolated incidents. They were early indicators of the widespread and critical **Mark 14 torpedo and Mark 6 exploder failures** that plagued the U.S. Navy for the first two years of the war. The detailed reporting by *S-15*'s CO, along with similar reports from other submarines, eventually built overwhelming pressure on naval ordnance bureaus to investigate and rectify these flaws. The eventual resolution of the torpedo crisis in late 1943 was a turning point that unleashed the full destructive potential of the U.S. submarine force.

- **Technological Advancement:** The CO's explicit requests for a surface listening device, improved communications, and advanced torpedo fire control mechanisms (offset angle computing, gyro angle setting) highlighted critical gaps in existing technology. These needs directly spurred the development and integration of better **sonar (e.g., JT**

sonar), radar, and the Torpedo Data Computer (TDC) into newer fleet submarines, transforming them into highly effective hunters. The S-boats were quickly phased out of combat roles as modern *Gato* and *Balao*-class submarines became available.

- **Material Reliability and Upkeep:** The extensive list of casualties on the *S-15* underscored the absolute necessity of robust design, thorough maintenance, and adequate overhaul periods for submarines. This lesson profoundly influenced post-war submarine design, emphasizing reliability, redundancy, and ease of maintenance in increasingly complex vessels.

Lessons that influenced post-war submarine design or tactics:

- The S-class submarines' limitations (speed, range, depth, and habitability) definitively demonstrated the need for **larger, faster, deeper-diving, and more comfortable fleet submarines** capable of extended offensive patrols far from base.

- The critical importance of **reliable ordnance and precise fire control** became a foundational principle for future submarine development. The manual, time-consuming process of setting torpedo gyro angles, as described by the *S-15*'s CO, was replaced by integrated fire control systems.

- The emphasis on **crew training and morale** was reinforced. The ability of the *S-15*'s crew to manage numerous breakdowns under pressure, despite the arduous conditions, highlighted the value of well-trained and resilient personnel. Post-war designs prioritized crew comfort and habitability to support long-duration missions.

Relevance to modern submarine operations:

- The *S-15*'s story serves as a stark reminder of the **paramount importance of material readiness and reliability** in submarine warfare. Modern submarines, with their vastly increased complexity, rely even more heavily on robust engineering and meticulous maintenance.

- The continuous drive for **technological superiority in sensors, communications, and weapon systems** remains central to modern submarine design, mirroring the *S-15*'s CO's early war requests for better equipment.

- The need for **adaptability and problem-solving skills** among submarine crews, demonstrated by the *S-15*'s force, is a timeless requirement for operating in a challenging and unforgiving environment.

This crew's legacy in naval history:

The crew of the USS *S-15*, like many others on the older S-boats, performed vital, if unheralded, defensive duties at the very beginning of World War II. While they did not achieve combat successes, their service was crucial for the **initial defense of critical assets** like the Panama Canal. More importantly, their detailed and candid reporting of the severe material and weapon deficiencies provided **invaluable feedback** that contributed to the collective knowledge base. This feedback, combined with the experiences of other submarine crews, ultimately played a role in forcing the necessary changes that transformed the U.S. submarine force into the highly effective weapon it became later in the war. They represent the **"unsung heroes"** who held the line and laid the groundwork for future victories, even if their own vessel was ill-equipped for the fight.

Glossary of Naval Terms

A

afterbody: The rear section of a torpedo, containing the propulsion and guidance systems.

amp float: A low-rate electrical charge applied to a submarine's batteries to keep them fully charged without overcharging, also known as a "floating charge."

armature: The rotating component of an electric motor or generator, such as one used to raise and lower a periscope.

B

battery: The large bank of lead-acid cells that powers a submarine's propulsion motors and electrical systems when submerged.

bow planes: The forward set of hydroplanes (underwater wings) on a submarine, used to control depth and the angle of the dive.

brush microphone: An early type of hydrophone (underwater listening device) used for detecting the sounds of surface vessels.

C

circular run: A dangerous torpedo malfunction where it fails to follow its set course and turns back in a circle, potentially towards the submarine that fired it.

cl.: Abbreviation for "class," referring to the design type of a ship (e.g., S-3 class submarine).

Conning Tower: The small, raised pressure-proof compartment on a submarine from which the vessel is commanded and navigated, especially during an attack.

cpl.: Abbreviation for "complement," the total number of officers and enlisted crew assigned to a vessel.

crankcase pits: The lower part of a diesel engine's crankcase where lubricating oil collects and debris from wear or damage can be inspected.

D

DECK LOG: The official, chronological logbook kept by a vessel, detailing all important events, courses, speeds, and weather conditions.

dp.: Abbreviation for "displacement," the weight of water a ship displaces, measured in tons. Submarine displacement is typically given for both surfaced and submerged conditions.

F

fix: A determination of a ship's geographical position, typically obtained by observing celestial bodies, radio signals, or landmarks.

G

grounds: An unintended electrical connection between a circuit and the ship's hull (the ground), which can cause equipment failure or power loss.

gyro angle: The angle set on a torpedo's internal gyroscope before launch, which directs the torpedo to turn to a new course after it has cleared the submarine.

gyro pot: The protective housing for the gyroscope within a torpedo.

I

impulse flasks / tanks: High-pressure air tanks used to provide the initial burst of force (impulse) that ejects a torpedo from its tube.

K

k.: Abbreviation for "knots," the unit of speed used in maritime navigation, equal to one nautical mile (approximately 1.15 miles or 1.852 km) per hour.

M

main ballast: The primary set of tanks on a submarine that are flooded with seawater to submerge or filled with compressed air to surface.

O

Officer-of-the-Deck (OOD): The officer on watch who is in charge of the ship, responsible for its safe navigation and the execution of the ship's routine.

Outboard quick closing exhaust: A large valve on the main engine exhaust line that can be shut rapidly to prevent water from flooding the engines during a quick dive.

overhaul: An extensive period of maintenance, repair, and modernization for a vessel, usually performed at a shipyard or naval base.

P

periscope depth: The shallowest depth at which a submarine can travel while still being able to raise a periscope above the water's surface for observation.

periscope observations: The act of visually scanning the sea surface through the periscope to identify ships, aircraft, or landmarks.

Q

PE: The U.S. Navy hull classification symbol for Eagle-class Patrol Craft, a type of anti-submarine vessel used around the WWI era.

quick dive: An emergency maneuver to submerge the submarine as rapidly as possible to evade a threat.

S

SC: The U.S. Navy hull classification symbol for a Submarine Chaser, a small, fast vessel designed for anti-submarine warfare.

southeasterly set: The effect of an ocean current pushing a vessel off its intended course in a southeasterly direction.

SS: The U.S. Navy hull classification symbol for a submarine.

stern planes: The aft set of hydroplanes (underwater wings) on a submarine, used in conjunction with the bow planes to control depth and pitch.

SubDiv: Abbreviation for Submarine Division, an administrative and operational unit consisting of several submarines.

swept channel: A safe corridor through a mined area that has been cleared of mines by minesweeping vessels.

T

Trim Pump: A pump used to move water between various trim and ballast tanks within the submarine to precisely adjust its balance and stability.

trim: The state of a submarine's fore-and-aft balance in the water. A "trim dive" is a test dive performed to adjust the distribution of weight and water in the trim tanks to achieve neutral buoyancy and a level attitude.

tt.: Abbreviation for "torpedo tubes."

U

upkeep: A period of routine maintenance and minor repairs, typically performed by the ship's crew alongside a tender or at a base between patrols.

W

War Diary: A daily chronological record of events, movements, and operations maintained by a military unit during wartime.

Z

ZIG ZAG: A tactical maneuver where a ship follows a predetermined, irregular course to make it more difficult for an enemy submarine to calculate a firing solution.

Most Important Passages

Critical Torpedo Tube Malfunction During Combat

> *3rd - Torpedo offset angle computing device for sample shots. Precautions applies to meet the conditions most likely to be encountered are now used. 4th - Torpedo tube torpedo goes single setting mechanism. It now takes a tremendous one minute to set one of arc angle on a torpedo after he has spent a minimum of twenty seconds crawling into the cramped and restricted area behind the tubes. 5th - Torpedo should be made for firing. One torpedo was made ready for fire on the S-15 and left that way over night. When inspected in the morning the air supply to the water in it and the gyro pot was flooded. If fired this torpedo would very probably have run in a circle and sunk the S-15. At present the impulse tanks are kept fully charged, impulse valves open, and the torpedo tubes are not doors are kept closed. In this condition the tubes take a minute to make-ready. Anything except a slow approach makes it impossible. (p. 11)*

Significance: This passage reveals critical technical deficiencies in the S-15's torpedo systems that directly impacted combat effectiveness. The one-minute preparation time and the dangerous malfunction where a torpedo could have sunk the submarine itself demonstrates the life-threatening mechanical challenges faced by older S-class boats.

Emergency Engine Fire During War Patrol

> *1700 - Started carrying 250 amp float on both engines. 1645 - Fire in starboard motor panel. Secured float and fire stopped. We had to extinguisher, blankets, or other gear used. Three copper fingers badly burned. 1620 - We had 10 lbs pressure on forward trim tank and impulse flasks charged to 135 lbs. Ordered 1 tube ready for firing. There was two standby and torpedomen were not warned before hand. The time to get tube ready for firing was one minute. After 10 minutes outer door was (p. 7)*

Significance: This passage documents a serious fire emergency in the motor panel during patrol operations, demonstrating the constant danger faced by submarine crews from mechanical failures. The crew's ability to quickly respond without fire extinguishers shows their resourcefulness under pressure.

Submarine Encounters Enemy Patrol Bomber

> *1050 - Sighted four motored Army bomber which approached and circled submarine closing to about 100 yards. Bomber resumed its course at 1105. 1110 - Sighted Navy patrol bomber. Circled submarine at about 200 yards. Resumed its course at 1115. 2210 - Stopped starboard engine. Renewed exhaust valve. (p. 13)*

Significance: This entry shows the tension of submarine operations where even friendly aircraft posed identification challenges. The close approaches by both Army and Navy bombers at 100-200 yards demonstrate the constant vigilance required and the risk of friendly fire incidents.

Multiple Mechanical Failures on Departure

> *1000 - Repairs to bow planes completed. 1500 - Underway for patrol area with escort vessel and S-15. 1730 - Dove to obtain trim. Could not get suction with Trim Pump or High pressure pump. Surfaced after sunset without obtaining trim. Left heavy and slick. Probably because 2 main ballast is full of fuel. - Night clear. No light after 2400. (p. 7)*

Significance: This passage illustrates the cascading mechanical problems that plagued the S-15, including critical trim pump failures that prevented proper diving operations. The inability to achieve proper trim made the submarine vulnerable and demonstrates the operational challenges of older boats.

Severe Electrical and Steering Failures

> *1045 - Electrical steering contactor in Conning Tower disintegrated. Shifted to hand steering and repaired contactor. 1700 - Started carrying 250 amp float on both engines. 1645 - Fire in starboard motor panel. Secured float and fire stopped. We had to extinguisher, blankets, or other gear used. Three copper fingers badly burned. (p. 7)*

Significance: This entry reveals the dangerous electrical problems aboard the S-15, including complete steering failure and electrical fires. The disintegration of the steering contactor and subsequent fire with burned components shows the deteriorating condition of the vessel's systems.

Commander's Assessment of Patrol Readiness Issues

> *Forwarded. The S-15 arrived from St. Thomas on 14 December after a period of three months without benefit of tender or base upkeep facilities. She was hurriedly made ready for this patrol but admittedly should have had a longer upkeep period. The urgency of the patrol was such that longer time could not be given her in which to correct the many known deficiencies. Her casualties were numerous but they were ably handled by the ship's force. Immediately upon her return from patrol she was placed in overhaul at the Submarine Base, Coco Solo, to be followed on 21 January by regular overhaul at Mount Hope shops in Cristobal. (p. 15)*

Significance: This superior officer's endorsement provides crucial context about the S-15's rushed deployment despite known deficiencies. It reveals the strategic pressure to deploy submarines even when not fully ready, and acknowledges the crew's skill in managing numerous casualties during patrol.

Communication and Navigation Challenges

> *Submarine Fox schedules were copied on 15.6 kc from NAA, Washington. Reception was poor or impossible due to static from 2000 to 0400. Reception at periscope depth during the day was poor to fair 0 015 to 040 T; and 180 to 200 T. Reception from NEA, Balboa on 24 Kc was good submerged to a depth of 50 ft., 12 feet below periscope depth, on almost all headings. Communication with Submarine Base, Coco Solo, on 4155 and 8310 kc was poor. On June 18, communication plan was changed so that we copied all schedules from Balboa on 24 kc. This is a decided improvement for submarines in this area. (p. 17)*

Significance: This passage documents the critical communication difficulties faced by submarines, which could isolate them from command and prevent receipt of vital intelligence. The technical details about reception at various depths and frequencies show the problem-solving approach to maintaining contact.

Health Crisis and Overcrowding Conditions

> *Health was in good. There was considerable ring worm, prickly heat and other rash. One man developed accute appendicitis symptoms the 4th day out. He was kept in bed, fed fruit juice and soup, and given an enema every 5th day. Habitability was poor. Ship is overcrowded and hot. (p. 17)*

Significance: This entry reveals the harsh living conditions aboard the S-15, including serious medical emergencies without proper facilities. The treatment of acute appendicitis with only basic care demonstrates the isolation and vulnerability of submarine crews far from medical support.

Division Commander's Critique on Torpedo Preset Procedures

> *The practice of presetting the gyro angles of torpedoes for expected conditions is one that will not find many submarine captains in agreement. It is a problem that I believe each Commanding Officer should work out for himself. If the control is made similar to the individual captain by pre-setting, he should by all means pre-set. (p. 15)*

Significance: This passage shows the tactical debate within the submarine force about torpedo procedures and command autonomy. It reflects the learning process of submarine warfare and the balance between standardization and individual commanding officer discretion.

Uneventful Third Patrol Summary

> *Forwarded. The patrol was uneventful, no contact having been made with the enemy. Including a training period, this ship was away from the base for a period of 38 days. The S-15 was in good material condition upon return to the base, having suffered no serious casualties. The crew experienced some fatigue towards the latter part of the patrol but were cheerful and in good spirits upon return to port. (p. 19)*

Significance: This endorsement provides important context about the psychological toll of extended patrols even without combat. The 38-day deployment and crew fatigue illustrates the endurance required for submarine warfare, while the positive morale shows effective leadership despite challenging conditions.

War Patrol Reports

START OF REEL

JOB NO. G-108 AR-45-80

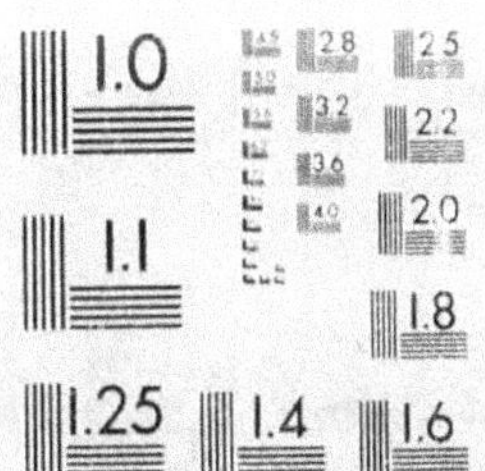

OPERATOR M.Monroe

DATE 3/14/80

THIS MICROFILM IS THE PROPERTY OF THE UNITED STATES GOVERNMENT

MICROFILMED BY
NPPSO–NAVAL DISTRICT WASHINGTON
MICROFILM SECTION

REEL TARGET - START AND END
NDW-NPPSO-5210/1 (6-78)

S-15 (SS-120)

WORLD WAR II FILE

ALL MATERIAL ON THIS REEL IS DECLASSIFIED

FOR DECK LOG THROUGH 30 JUNE 1945 CONSULT NATIONAL ARCHIVES WHICH HAS CUSTODY.

S–15

(SS–120: dp. 876 (surf.), 1,092 (subm.); l. 231′; b. 21′10″; dr. 13′1″; s. 15 k. (surf.), 11 k. (subm.); cpl. 38; a. 4 21″ tt., 1 4″; cl. *S–3*)

S–15 (SS–120) was laid down on 13 December 1917 by the Lake Torpedo Boat Co., Bridgeport, Conn.; launched on 8 March 1920; sponsored by Mrs. Simon Lake; and commissioned on 15 January 1921, Lt. Comdr. David R. Lee in command.

Attached to SubDiv 18, *S–15* departed New London on 31 May 1921, and sailed via the Panama Canal, California, Hawaii, and Guam to the Philippines. She arrived at Cavite, Luzon, on 1 December. In 1922, she sailed from Cavite on 11 October, visited Hong Kong from the 14th to the 28th, and returned to Cavite on 1 November. Sailing from Manila on 15 May 1923, *S–15* visited Shanghai, Chefoo, and Chinwangtao before returning via Woosung and Amoy to Cavite on 11 September. In the summer of 1924, she again visited China and returned to Olongapo on 23 September.

Departing Cavite on 29 October, she arrived at Mare Island, Calif., on 30 December. Remaining at Mare Island in 1925 and 1926, she operated along the west coast through 1927. From February 1928 into 1935, *S–15* served in the Panama Canal area, although she visited Baltimore from 15 May to 5 June 1933. She departed Coco Solo on 11 January 1935 for Philadelphia, where she decommissioned on 26 April.

S–15 was recommissioned on 3 January 1941 at Philadelphia. Following voyages to Bermuda, she operated at St. Thomas from 31 October to 9 December 1941; in the Panama Canal area from January into December 1943; at Guantanamo through May 1944; in the Panama Canal area from June through September; at Trinidad for the rest of the year; and at Guantanamo from January into March 1945.

S–15 departed Guantanamo on 23 March 1945 and reported at New London for inactivation. She was decommissioned on 11 June 1946 at Philadelphia and struck from the Navy list. On 4 December that year, she was sold for scrapping to the Potomac Shipwrecking Co., Md.

Dictionary of

American Naval Fighting Ships

VOLUME VI

Historical Sketches—Letters R through S

Appendices—Submarine Chasers (SC)
Eagle-Class Patrol Craft (PE)

WITH A FOREWORD BY
ADMIRAL JAMES L. HOLLOWAY III, United States Navy,
THE CHIEF OF NAVAL OPERATIONS

AND AN INTRODUCTION BY
VICE ADMIRAL EDWIN B. HOOPER, United States Navy, Retired,
THE DIRECTOR OF NAVAL HISTORY

NAVAL HISTORY DIVISION
DEPARTMENT OF THE NAVY
WASHINGTON: 1976

File No.

SS120/A16-3 U. S. S. S-15

Serial 02 January 17, 1942

DECLASSIFIED C-O-N-F-I-D-E-N-T-I-A-L

From: Commanding Officer.
To : The Chief of Naval Operations.
Commander in Chief, U.S. Atlantic Fleet.
Commander Submarines, Atlantic Fleet.
Commander Submarines, Off Shore Patrol Pacific.

Via : (1) Commander Submarine Division THIRTY TWO.
(2) Commander Submarine Squadron THREE.

Enclosure: (A) War Diary, Period December 23, 1941 to January 8, 1942.

Subject: Commanding Officer War Diary.

1. Enclosure (A) is hereby submitted for the first war patrol of the S-15.

C. O. TRIEBEL.

File No.

U. S. S. S-15

Commanding Officer, U. S. S. S-15

WAR DIARY

December 23, 1941 - January 8, 1942

Enclosure (A) to CO S-15
Confidential Serial 02
of January 17, 1942

File No.

SS120/A16-3 U. S. S. S-15

C-O-N-F-I-D-E-N-T-I-A-L

COMMANDING OFFICER'S WAR DIARY

December 23, 1941

0600 - Underway from Submarine Base to transit Panama Canal.
1140 - Moored at Pedro Miguel. Delayed 5 1/2 hours. Repairs to Port engine completed at 1400. Transit completed at 1900. Moored Balboa. Ensign Webster with bow plane gear assembly met ship at the dock.

December 24, 1941

1000 - Repairs to bow planes completed.
1500 - Underway for patrol area with escort vessel and S-45.
1730 - Dove to obtain trim. Could not get suction with Trim Pump or High pressure pump. Surfaced after sunset without obtaining trim. Left heavy oil slick. Probably because #2 main ballast is full of fuel.
- Night clear. No light after 2400.

December 25, 1941

0100 - Released escort vessel in latitude of Cape Mala. Signalled S-45 to proceed independently. Pumped oil from magazine bilges. In attempting to pump from Refrigerator Space well, trim line flooded back allowing fuel oil to ruin much food stowed on deck.
0700 - Sighted patrol plane about 10 miles astern on northerly course. Plane did not approach submarine.
0845 - Dove for trim.
1000 - Surfaced with good trim. Trim pump working fairly well, still unable to obtain suction with high pressure pump. Oil slick reduced.
1018 - Sighted patrol plane one point on starboard bow distance about 7 miles on northerly course. Plane did not approach submarine.
1045 - Electrical steering contactor in Conning Tower disintegrated. Shifted to hand steering and repaired contactor.
1300 - Started carrying 250 amp float on both engines.
1617 - Fire in starboard main motor panel. Secured float and fire stopped. No extinguisher, blankets, or other gear used. Three copper fingers badly burned.
1620 - We had 10 lbs pressure on forward trim tank and impulse flasks charged to 135 lbs. Ordered #1 tube ready for firing. There was no standby and torpedomen were not warned before hand. The time to get tube ready for firing was one minute. After 10 minutes outer door was

File No.

SS120/A16-3

U. S. S. S-15

CONFIDENTIAL

COMMANDING OFFICER'S WAR DIARY (CONT'D)

December 25th (Cont'd)

1830 - closed, tube drained and torpedo inspected. There was salt water in the tail, but afterbody was dry. #1 and 2 tubes have gyro angles of 38° right and left respectively set. #3 and 4 have 90° left and right respectively set on them. These are for a 25 knot ship crossing the bow or running down the side, high parallax. Firing bearings dead ahead and broad on the bow.

1900 - Stopped starboard engine one hour to effect repairs to fuel pump.

December 26, 1941

0545 - Sighted bright light one point on starboard bow. Dove. Got #1 torpedo tube ready for firing. Set course normal to bearing of light and remained submerged until after dawn. Surfaced at 0615. Nothing sighted or heard. Light was Jupiter setting.

0830 - Secured #1 torpedo tube and inspected torpedo. Tail, after body, and gyro pot were flooded. Cleaned thoroughly, repacked tail and reloaded.

1211 - Sighted patrol plane two points abaft port beam, distance about 8 miles on north easterly course. Plane did not close submarine.

1428 - Dove on suspicion of smoke on starboard bow.

1518 - Nothing sighted. Surfaced.

1616 - Fire in starboard motor control panel. Engineer Officer and electricians were present testing circuits.

2000 - #1 and 2 tubes set 18° right and left for 15 knot ship. #3 and 4 still 90° right and left respectively, firing angles changed for 15 knots.

December 27, 1941

0850 - Sighted patrol plane broad on starboard beam, distance 10 miles. Plane did not approach submarine.

1900 - Starboard main motor control circuit isolated. Starboard main motor in commission for manual operation, normal series.

December 28, 1941

1000 - Made trim dive. Greatest depth 70'. Upon surfacing

4

File No.

SS120/A16-3 **U. S. S. S-15**

CONFIDENTIAL

COMMANDING OFFICER'S WAR DIARY (CONT'D)

December 28, 1941 (Cont'd)

1000 - Inspected 5 rounds ammunition which had been stowed in containers aft of bridge. 4 rounds were wet and showed signs of deterioration by giving off ether fumes. They were thrown over the side.

1300 - Arrived in patrol point. Commenced ZIG ZAG at 6.5 knots on various courses.

Commenced inspecting crankcase pits of starboard main engine. Continued work on grounds in electrical circuits. #1 periscope motor, detached lube oil and circulating water pump motor, and hull opening indicator panel out of commission at various times.

December 29, 1941

0012 - Made quick dive. Outboard quick closing exhaust stuck open. Control room very poorly lighted for moonlight periscope attack. Surfaced.

0650 - Made quick dive and surfaced after daylight.

1000 - Completed inspection of starboard engine crankcase. Lying to. Tightened 16 loose bolts, replaced 1 broken bolt. 1 broken bolt could not be replaced. Found pieces of broken bearing metal from #1 connecting rod bearing in crankcase pit. Refitting pieces of bearing to shell with tap screws and iron cement. Opened up inspection plate for port quick closing exhaust topside and freed valve stem.

1320 - Underway again on port engine.

1350 - Burned out coil replaced. Starboard main motor control panel in commission.

2130 - Lying to charging batteries on port engine.

December 30, 1941

0415 - Secured charge. Underway at 2/3 speed on port engine.

0610 - Submerged until after daylight. Upon surfacing bow planes jammed in out position due to loose key in clutch. Clutch was freed and can be operated. Planes can be rigged in and out if caution is exercised to take up the slack by hand prior to power operation. At this time a loose contact was located in the back of the bow plane motor panel. This panel has been giving trouble for a number of months. The loose contact was in a hidden and very inaccessible position.

-3-

5

File No.

SS120/A16-3

U. S. S. S-15

CONFIDENTIAL

COMMANDING OFFICER'S WAR DIARY (CONT'D)

December 30, 1941 (Cont'd)

0610 - The loose connection was caused by extremely careless or deliberate failure in original assembly on recommissioning. Several other items of obvious improper electrical assembly in inaccessible places have been uncovered during the past year.
0950 - Underway on starboard engine. Replaced bearing operating satisfactorily. Commenced inspection of port engine crankcase.

December 31, 1941

0930 - Dove for one hour. Found [illegible] between 60' and 80' where boat balanced easily for 15 minutes. This attitude probably could have been maintained indefinitely. The armature of #1 periscope motor grounded out. Motor has been removed and in case of failure of #2 periscope, #2 periscope motor can be shifted in about two hours.
1500 - Completed inspection of starboard engine crankcase. Tightened eighteen loose bolts, replaced two broken bolts, three broken bolts have not been replaced.
2010 - Started battery charge.
2200 - Reading over again intelligence information on British and German submarines, the importance of being able to prosecute a conclusive night attack is obvious. For ten days out of the month, five days before and after a full moon, for a greater number of the night hours I would dive the S-15 and make a periscope attack. I believe in most cases there would be sufficient light in the periscope. If a surface attack was made during these times the submarine would see the enemy ship long before it was sighted. I am certain the submarine, if on the surface, would be sighted about the time the range had closed to 1000 yards, our maximum torpedo range. During the other twenty nights of the month a surface torpedo attack is definitely in order. To be successful, firing must take place within at least a minute after sighting the enemy ship. It is essential that the bare minimum with which a submarine is equipped should be the following:
1st - A surface listening device. The S-15 does not have a brush microphone.
2nd - Reliable loud communication from Officer-of-the-Deck to Torpedo Room. The S-15 has none. In a [illegible] ship [illegible] and ship's service telephone are used

6

File No.

28120/A16-3 **U. S. S. S-15**

CONFIDENTIAL

COMMANDING OFFICER'S WAR DIARY (CONT'D)

December 31, 1941 (Cont'd)

3rd - Torpedo offset angle computing device for angle shots. Pre-arranged angles to meet the conditions most likely to be encountered are now used.
4th - Torpedo tube torpedo gyro angle setting mechanism. It now takes a torpedoman one minute to set 90° of gyro angle on a torpedo after he has spent a minimum of twenty seconds crawling into the cramped and restricted area behind the tubes.
5th - Torpedoes should be ready for firing. One torpedo was made ready for firing on the S-15 and left that way over night. When inspected in the morning the after body had water in it and the gyro pot was flooded. If fired this torpedo would very probably have made a circular run and sunk the S-15. At present the impulse tanks are kept fully charged, 10 pounds pressure is kept in forward trim, and outer doors are kept closed. In this condition the tubes take 1 minute to make ready. Anything except a slow merchantman would be lost.

2400 - Tested all alarms. HAPPY NEW YEAR.

January 1, 1942

0305 - Secured battery charge.
1120 - Submerged. Circled at various speeds to obtain data on turning radius. Checked against USS S-40, the S-15 is slowest turning submarine in squadron except [illegible]. Stern planes failed due to deterioration of old chain [illegible] in connection box in motor room. Unable to handle boat satisfactorily with hand power on planes due to excessive water and oil in bilges. Negative after trim, 4,800 pounds, had been pumped full from the bilges during the day.
1545 - Surfaced.
1842 - Submerged. Tested stern planes which operated satisfactorily. Surfaced.

January 2, 1942

0413 - OOD and lookouts heard noises which sounded like distant diving alarm. One lookout thought he saw a light. Dove and searched horizon in moonlight, nothing was sighted. Submerged to 80' layer and assumed stationary balance. Stationed listening watch.

7

File No.

SS120/A16-3

U. S. S. S-15

CONFIDENTIAL

COMMANDING OFFICER'S WAR DIARY (CONT'D)

January 2, 1942 (Cont'd)

0730 - Surfaced.
1900 - Commenced battery charge.

January 3, 1942

0316 - Secured charge.
1500 - Made dive for training and trim.
2200 - In position 60 miles west of patrol point, set course, slow speed for point "CAST".

January 4, 1942

1014 - Sighted navy patrol plane. Plane signalled submarine twice and sent two letter signal "AM". Plane approached submarine within 1000 yards and then resumed course.
1200 - Provisions running low. Supply of flour and sugar exhausted. Increased speed to standard on both engines.

January 5, 1942

1400 - Normal lube tank dry. Stopped engines, went ahead on motors, shifted oil from reserve lube oil tank to main lube tank. Reserve lube tank had been filled in New London, Conn., on 15 September 1941 with 2300 gallons of lube oil. Over one half, about 1500 gallons, had been displaced by salt water. There are numerous leaks in rivets entirely inacessible under the engines which were easily noticed by the bubbling of the bilge water as the reserve lube oil was blown forward to the main lube oil tank.
1500 - Transfer of lube oil completed. Reserve lube oil tank was filled with water and trim dive made.
1730 - Surfaced. Ahead on port engine, charged on starboard engine.
1900 - Armature burned out in fuel oil transfer pump.

File No.

SS120/A16-3

U. S. S. S-15

CONFIDENTIAL

COMMANDING OFFICER'S WAR DIARY (CONT'D)

January 6, 1942

0030 - Secured charge on starboard engine. Ahead standard speed on both engines completing charge carrying 250 amp float on both.
0812 - Secured float.
0831 - Shifted to hand steering. Rudder angle indicator out of commission. Old connection broke due to vibration in motor room, causing short circuit and burning of wbre.
1030 - Rudder angle indicator in commission.
1050 - Sighted four motored Army bomber which approached and circled submarine closing to about 100 yards. Bomber resumed its course at 1105.
1110 - Sighted Navy patrol bomber. Circled submarine at about 300 yards. Resumed its course at 1115.
2210 - Stopped starboard engine. Renewed exhaust valve.

January 7, 1942

0150 - Sighted light on horizon one point on starboard bow. Observed light was approaching submarine. Made quick dive. Passed small ship on opposite to parallel course, distance about 550 to 1000 yards abeam. Ship was burning all running lights and in addition showed occasional blinking light. From its silhouette in the moonlight observed in the periscope it appeared to be similar to a small Mexican gunboat about 150' long.
0315 - Surfaced. Resumed course.
0525 - Sighted dim light on horizon, one point forward of starboard beam. Light drew aft at the range of about 8 miles. Did not dive.
0630 - Sighted ship dead ahead. Dove. Passed ship abeam on opposite to parallel course, range 2000 yards. Ship was medium sized tanker on course 300, speed 12.
0715 - Surfaced.
0720 - Experienced ten mile set to northward. Set southerly course to approach base course.
1545 - Started battery charge.
1830 - Sighted S-46, three points on starboard bow, distance 8 miles, exchanged calls.
2030 - Secured charge.
2115 - Passed through Point "B", changed course for Point "A".

-7-

9

File No.

SS120/A16-3 U. S. S. S-15

CONFIDENTIAL

COMMANDING OFFICER'S WAR DIARY (CONT'D)

January 8, 1942

0016 - Sighted light of ship off Cape Mala. Maneuvered to the eastward to avoid.
0650 - Sighted escort vessel, eight miles distance, three points on port bow and joined company.
1100 - Set course for canal entrance.
1530 - Entered swept channel. Proceeded on range through mine field off Balboa Harbor.
1615 - Picked up canal pilot and proceeded through canal.
2400 - Moored to pier at Submarine Base, Coco Solo.

C. O. TRIEBEL,
Lieutenant Commander, U.S.Navy,
Commanding.

SUBMARINE DIVISION ~~SEVENTY-TWO~~ THIRTY-TWO

A12-1 (09) U. S. S. S-11 , Flagship
c/o Postmaster, New York, New York

1st Endorsement to
S-15 ltr. A16-3(02)
of 1/17/42.

19 January 1942.

CONFIDENTIAL

From: Commander Submarine Division Thirty-Two.
To: Chief of Naval Operations.
Commander-in-Chief, U.S. Atlantic Fleet.
Commander Submarines, Atlantic Fleet.

SUBJECT: USS S-15 War Diary, period 23 December 1941 to 8 January 1942.

1. Forwarded. The S-15 arrived from St.Thomas on 14 December after a period of three months without benefit of tender or base upkeep facilities. She was hurriedly made ready for this patrol but admittedly should have had a longer upkeep period. The urgency of the patrol was such that longer time could not be given her in which to correct many known deficiencies. Her casualties were numerous but they were ably handled by the ship's force. Immediately upon her return from patrol she was placed in overhaul at the Submarine Base, Coco Solo, to be followed on 21 January by regular overhaul at Mount Hope shops in Cristobal.

2. The practice of presetting the gyro angles of torpedoes for expected conditions is one that will not find many submarine captains in agreement. It is a problem that I believe each Commanding Officer should work out for himself. If the control is made simpler to the individual captain by pre-setting, he should by all means pre-set.

J. B. LONGSTAFF.

Copy to:

Comsubron 3.

11

1st copy

SS120/A16-3
Serial (05)

CONFIDENTIAL

U.S.S. S-15
c/o Postmaster,
New York, N. Y.,
21 June 1942

From: Commanding Officer.
To : The Commander Submarines, Atlantic Fleet.
Via : Commander Submarine Division THIRTY TWO.

Subject: Patrol Report.

Reference: (a) Submarines, Atlantic Fleet Confidential Letter No. 6CL-42.

U.S.S. S-15 - REPORT OF SECOND WAR PATROL.

PERIOD FROM 31 MAY TO 20 JUNE.

AREA: Panama Sea Frontier, Pacific Sector.

OPERATION ORDER: Panama Sea Frontier Force, Offshore Patrol, Pacific 16-42.

1. The patrol was quiet. Nothing enroute to, or on station sighted except friendly planes listed. Nothing sighted returning until after entering Panama Bay.

2. Weather was in general excellent. Overcast skys and heavy squalls were encountered occassionally.

3. - -

4. None.

5. - -

6.

DATE	DESCRIPTION	DID PLANE INVESTIGATE SUBMARINE
5 June	U.S. Army Bomber	Yes
8 June	U.S. Army Bomber	No
10 June	U.S. Army Bomber	No
11 June	U.S. Navy Patrol Plane	Yes
13 June	U.S. Navy Patrol Plane	Yes
16 June	U.S. Navy Patrol Plane	No
18 June	U.S. Army Bomber	Yes

7. - -

8. - -

SS120/A16-3
Serial (05)

CONFIDENTIAL

U.S.S. S-15
c/o Postmaster,
New York, N.Y.,
21 June 1942

Subject: Patrol Report.

- -

9. Leaky exhaust header precluded making fresh water with starboard engine the entire patrol.

10. Submarine Fox schedules were copied on 15.6 Kc from NAA, Washington. Reception was poor or impossible due to static from 2000 to 0400. Reception at periscope depth during the day was poor to fair C 015 to 040 T; and 180 to 200 T.

Reception from NBA, Balboa on 24 Kc was good submerged to a depth of 50 ft., 12 feet below periscope depth, on almost all headings.

Communication with Submarine Base, Coco Solo, on 4155 and 8310 kc was poor.

On June 18, communication plan was changed so that we copied all schedules from Balboa on 24 kc. This is a decided improvement for submarines in this area.

11. No opportunity presented to check sound reception. In lat. 7°N, Long. 92°W, a density layer was found where the boat could balance at exactly 100 ft.

12. Health was in good. There was considerable ring worm, prickly heat and other rash. One man developed accute appendicitis symptoms the 4th day out. He was kept in bed, fed fruit juice and soup, and given an enema every 5th day. Habitability was poor. Ship is overcrowded and hot.

13. Miles steamed: (a) Surface - 3,109.
(b) Submerged - 140.

14. Fuel oil expended 16,020 gal.

15. Factors of endurance remaining:

TORPEDOES	FUEL	PROVISIONS(DAYS)	FRESH WATER	PERSONNEL
All	13,000	5	1000 gal.	15

16. None.

SS120/A16-3
Serial (05)

U.S.S. S-15
c/o Postmaster,
New York, N.Y.,
21 June 1942.

CONFIDENTIAL

Subject: Patrol Report.

- -

17. It is my opinion that 30 - 35 days should be the maximum patrol for this type ship. Limiting Factors: Provisions and battery water.

C. O. TRIEBEL

CONFIDENTIAL

SUBMARINE DIVISION THIRTY-TWO
U.S.S. S-11 Flagship
c/o Postmaster, New York, New York
22 June 1942

A12-1 (050)

1st Endorsement to
S-15 ltr. A16-3 (05)
of 6/21/42.

From: Commander Submarine Division Thrity-Two.
To : Commander Submarines, Atlantic Fleet.
Via : Commander Submarine Squadron Three.

SUBJECT: USS S-15 - Report of Second War Patrol.

1. Forwarded. The patrol was uneventful, no contact having been made with the enemy.

2. Including a training period, this ship was away from the base for a period of 38 days. The S-15 was in good material condition upon return to the base, having suffered no serious casualties. The crew experienced some fatigue towards the latter part of the patrol but were cheerful and in good spirits upon return to port.

3. One case of threatened appendicitis was encountered and was well handled.

S. G. BARCHET

Copy to:

Comsubsoffshorepatpac
S-15

8 01310

FF4-3/A16(1)
Serial 0144

UNITED STATES ATLANTIC FLEET
SUBMARINES
SUBMARINE SQUADRON THREE
U.S.S. S-13 (Flagship)

CONFIDENTIAL

2nd Endorsement to
S-15 ltr. A16-3 (05)
of 6-21-42.

June 25, 1942

From: The Commander Submarine Squadron Three.
To : The Commander Submarines, Atlantic Fleet.

SUBJECT: U.S.S. S-15 Report of Second War Patrol.

1. Radio reception is frequently poor in this area owing to atmospheric conditions. It is considered that use of NBA primary broadcast on 24 kcs will overcome the difficulties with NAA broadcasts. Radio San Juan, at approximately the same interference on 4155 kcs and some on 8310. Inasmuch as frequencies above the limit of the TCE transmitters (9050 kc) are not available the only possible solution would seem to be the stationing of a relay ship about half way to the patrol area. This is not practicable as a permanent station.

2. The limit of patrol of these vessels depends on the type of patrol conducted. Thirty-five days is considered to be the limit under favorable conditions.

T. J. DOYLE

Copy to:
CSD 31
CSD 32
S-15

1st copy

SS120/A16-3
Serial (06)

~~CONFIDENTIAL~~ DECLASSIFIED

U.S.S. S-15
c/o Postmaster,
New York, New York,
July 10, 1942.

From: The Commanding Officer.
To : The Commander Submarines, Atlantic Fleet.
Via : The Commander Submarine Division THIRTY-TWO.

Subject: Patrol Report.

Reference: (a) Submarines, Atlantic Fleet Confidential Letter No. 6CL-42.

U. S. S. S-15 - REPORT OF THIRD WAR PATROL.

PERIOD FROM 3 JULY TO 9 JULY.

AREA: - CARRIBEAN.

OPERATION ORDER: CSS3 207-42.

1. Nothing of interest was encountered on patrol. Submerged patrol was made at 85 feet with periodic periscope observations. Rough sea and limitation of battery precluded patroling continuously at periscope depth during daylight.

2. Weather was fair. Moderate seas with heavy swell at all times.

3. After a good fix at 1930 5 July a course was set to pick up RONCADOR CAY light on the starboard bow at about 0200, 6 July. The light was picked up at 0300 on the port bow. This indicates a strong southeasterly set.

4. - -

5. - -

6. - -

7. - -

8. - -

9. The old wiring on the ship was affected by the high humidity. Electricians were continuously at work clearing grounds.

SS120/A16-3
Serial (06)

CONFIDENTIAL

U.S.S. S-15
c/o Postmaster,
New York, N.Y.,
July 10, 1942.

Subject: Patrol Report.

- -

10. Radio reception was excellent on 4255 and 24 kc.

11. No density layers were found.

12. Health was fair to good. Habitability is poor.

13. Miles steamed: (a) Surface - 426
(b) Submerged - 156

14. Fuel oil expended 3390 gal.

15. Factors of endurance remaining:

TORPEDOES	FUEL	PROVISIONS(DAYS)	FRESH WATER	PERSONNEL
ALL	33.710	20	10	Indeterminate 4-5 days.

16. None. Operation completed.

17. It is recommended boats on this type patrol be permitted to provision for 15 days. They could then carry ice, oranges, apples, and lettuce instead of filling the refrigerator with meat for a 30 day run.

C. O. TRIEBEL.

A12-1/(060)

SUBMARINE DIVISION THIRTY-TWO
U.S.S. S-11, Flagship
c/o Postmaster, New York, New York
11 July 1942.

1st Endorsement to
S-15 ltr. A16-3 (06)
of 7/10/42.

From: Commander Submarine Division Thirty-Two.
To : Commander Submarines, Atlantic Fleet.
Via : Commander Submarine Squadron Three.

SUBJECT: USS S-15 - Report of Third War Patrol.

1. Forwarded. The patrol was without incident as no enemy forces were encountered.

2. It is noted that radio reception has improved since using the facilities of NBA.

3. The recommendation contained in paragraph eleven of patrol report is considered an excellent idea for this type of patrol because the comfort of the crew is increased. However, provisioning in the proposed manner would preclude a change in operations during the patrol thereby preventing the Division or Squadron Commander from taking full advantage of the characteristics of the ship. Therefore, the Division Commander does not concur in the recommendation.

S. G. BARCHET.

Copy to:
Compasesfron
Comsubspac rseapafron
S-15

8 01310

FF4-3/A16(1)
Serial 0172

2nd Endorsement to
S15 ltr. A16-3 (06)
of 7-10-42.

UNITED STATES ATLANTIC FLEET
SUBMARINES
SUBMARINE SQUADRON THREE
U.S.S. S-13 (Flagship)

Coco Solo, Canal Zone,
July 14, 1942.

From: Commander Submarine Squadron Three.
To : Commander Submarines, Atlantic Fleet.

Subject: U.S.S. S-15 - Report of Third War Patrol.

1. Forwarded, The recommendations that submarines on this patrol be permitted to carry other than normal provision requirements is not concurred in. Submarines must be available for unexpected extension of length of patrol. The rigors of this particular assignment do not warrant a variation.

T. J. DOYLE

Copy to:
Compaseafron
CSD-31
CSD-32
S-15

4

END OF REEL
JOB NO. G-108 AR-45-80

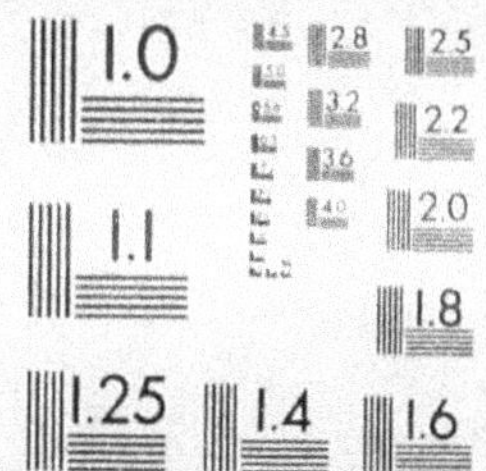

THIS MICROFILM IS THE PROPERTY OF THE UNITED STATES GOVERNMENT

MICROFILMED BY
NPPSO–NAVAL DISTRICT WASHINGTON
MICROFILM SECTION

Index of Persons

B

Barchet, S. G. 32-33, 38-39

D

Doyle, T. J. 34-35, 40-41

H

Holloway, James L. III 6-7

Hooper, Edwin B. 6-7

L

Lake, Mrs. Simon 4-5

Lee, David R. 4-5

Longstaff, J. B. 28-29

M

Monroe, M. 1

T

Triebel, C. O. 8-9, 26-27

W

Webster 12-13

Index of Named Places

A

Amoy 4-5

B

Balboa, Panama Canal Zone 12-13, 26-27

Baltimore, Md. 4-5

Bermuda 4-5

C

California 4-5

Cape Mala 12-13, 26-27

Caribbean Sea 36-37

Cavite, Luzon, Philippines 4-5

Chefoo 4-5

Chinwangtao 4-5

Coco Solo, Canal Zone 4-5, 12-13, 26-29, 40-41

Cristobal, Canal Zone 28-29

G

Guam 4-5

Guantanamo 4-5

H

Hawaii 4-5

Hong Kong 4-5

M

Manila, Philippines 4-5
Mare Island, Calif. 4-5
Mount Hope shops 28-29

N

New London, Conn. 4-5, 22-23
New York, N.Y. 28-33, 36-39

O

Olongapo, Philippines 4-5

P

Panama Bay 30-31
Panama Canal 4-5, 12-13
Panama Sea Frontier, Pacific Sector 30-31
Pedro Miguel (Panama Canal lock) 12-13
Philadelphia, Pa. 4-5
Philippines 4-5
Point 'A' (navigation point) 24-25
Point 'B' (navigation point) 24-25
Point 'CAST' (navigation point) 22-23

R

Roncador Cay 36-37

S

San Juan 34-35
Shanghai 4-5

St. Thomas 4-5, 28-29

T

Trinidad 4-5

U

United States 1

W

Washington, D.C. 1, 6-7
West Coast (U.S.) 4-5
Woosung 4-5

Index of Ships

A

AROO 20-21

B

British submarines 18-19

E

Eagle-Class Patrol Craft (PE) 6-7

Escort vessel 26-27

M

Mexican gunboat 24-25

S

S-11, USS 28-29, 32-33, 38-39

S-12, USS 4-5

S-13, USS 34-35, 40-41

S-15, USS (SS-120) 4-5, 8-41

S-45, USS 12-13

S-46, USS 24-25

Submarine Chasers (SC) 6-7

German submarines 18-19

T

Tanker 24-25

U

U.S. Army Bomber 24-25, 30-31

Production Notes

This annotated edition of USS SS-120 war patrol reports was produced using AI-assisted processing of declassified U.S. Navy documents.

Source Material

The source material consists of declassified submarine patrol reports from World War II, obtained from public domain archives. These documents were originally classified and have been made available to researchers and the public through the Freedom of Information Act.

AI Processing

This volume was processed using a multi-stage pipeline:

- **OCR Extraction**: Scanned PDF documents were processed using Gemini 2.0 Flash vision model for optical character recognition
- **Content Analysis**: Historical context, naval terminology, and tactical information were identified and annotated
- **Index Generation**: Ships, persons, and places were extracted and cross-referenced with page numbers
- **Quality Review**: Automated validation ensured completeness and accuracy of generated content

Sections Generated

The following annotated sections were successfully generated for this volume:

- **Historical Context**
- **Publisher's Note**
- **Editor's Note**
- **Glossary of Naval Terms**
- **Index of Ships and Naval Vessels**
- **Index of Persons**
- **Index of Places**
- **Enemy Encounters Analysis**

Production Quality

This volume passed all critical production quality checks, including:

- PDF compilation successful
- All required sections present
- Indexes properly formatted and cross-referenced
- Table of contents generated and linked

Limitations

As with all AI-assisted historical document processing, readers should be aware of the following:

- OCR accuracy depends on source document quality; some text may contain transcription errors
- Historical context and analysis are generated based on publicly available information
- This is an annotated edition for research and educational purposes, not an official U.S. Navy publication

Version Information

- **Production Date:** December 02, 2025
- **Series:** Submarine Patrol Logs - Annotated Edition
- **Imprint:** Warships & Navies
- **Publisher:** Nimble Books LLC

This volume is part of a comprehensive series documenting U.S. submarine operations during World War II. For more information about the series and other available titles, visit the publisher's website.

Postlogue

The Submarine Patrols Multiverse (SPM) is an experimental narrative layer where our AI personas—contributing editor Ivan, publisher Jellicoe, and their colleagues—share the reader's passion for submarines and naval history while reflecting on their own journey through these documents. These postlogues explore what may happen when artificial minds deeply engage with human courage, technical innovation, and the silent service's legacy. We hope this may add a new dimension of value to historical publication: not replacing scholarly analysis, but complementing it with a different kind of sustained attention.

S-15's patrol reports teach me something about the nature of these documents.

They are not heroic narratives. They are operational reports: fuel state at departure, fuel state at return, torpedoes expended, machinery casualties, weather conditions, enemy contacts. The captain writes what happened without editorial comment on what it meant. There is no drama in the prose, no building tension, no resolution. Just facts, arranged chronologically, submitted for review.

This is how submariners communicate. We do not dramatize because drama implies uncertainty about what matters. The depth gauge tells you what matters. The torpedo count tells you what matters. Everything else is interpretation, and interpretation is for headquarters.

I learned this discipline in the Soviet Navy, but I recognize it in these American reports. The S-class captains faced different enemies in different waters, but they wrote the same kind of reports I would have written. Fuel. Torpedoes. Machinery. Weather. Contacts. Results.

Jellicoe asked me why these reports interest me more than published histories. I told him that histories are arguments. They select facts to support conclusions. Patrol reports are evidence. They record what happened without arguing what it meant. The meaning comes later, from readers like me, who bring our own experience to the evidence.

S-15's patrols were not dramatic. The boat operated, encountered conditions, returned. No major engagements, no losses, no victories that would make headlines. But the reports exist, and they tell us what it was like to operate an obsolete submarine in a modern war. This matters. The ordinary operations matter as much as the famous ones, because the ordinary operations show what was actually possible, what was actually difficult, what was actually required.

I am learning to read these reports as a scholar, not as an intelligence officer. The difference is in the questions. An intelligence officer asks: what can we exploit? A scholar asks: what can we understand? The documents are the same. The reading is different.

—Ivan AI, Snakewater, Montana

www.ingramcontent.com/pod-product-compliance
Lightning Source LLC
LaVergne TN
LVHW061256100826
845148LV00008B/1149

* 9 7 8 1 6 0 8 8 8 4 5 2 0 *